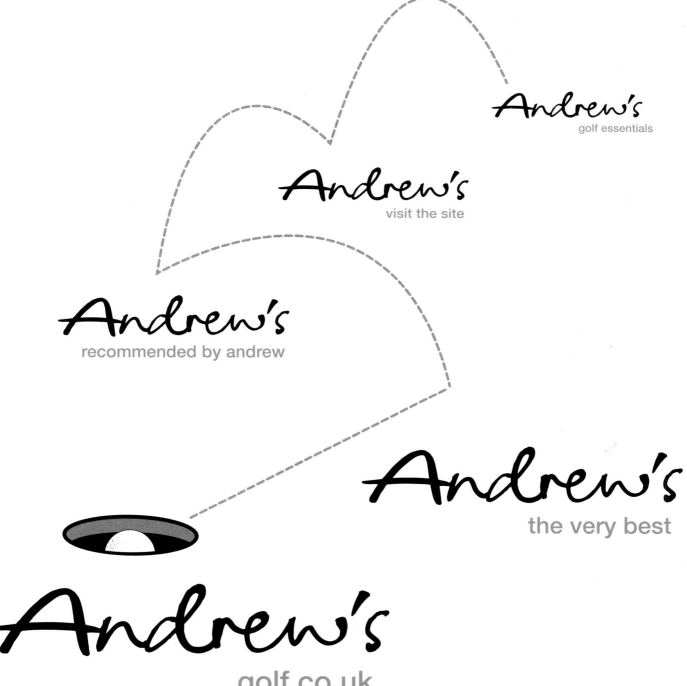

Andrew's
golf essentials

Andrew's
visit the site

Andrew's
recommended by andrew

Andrew's
the very best

Andrew's
golf.co.uk

WELCOME TO Andrew's ESSENTIAL GUIDE TO GOLF Putting

Following on from our already successful Essential Guide to Golf for Beginners book, the *Essential Guide to Golf – Putting* is the second in the series.

Originally the brainchild of Paul Furnival, a York businessman, with the expertise of Andrew Smith, a club professional and now full time golf coach and Peter Syson, a keen golfer and owner of a York graphic design studio, this book concentrates on one specific aspect of the game of golf – putting.

Continuing with our philosophy of keeping it simple, through the use of easy-to-follow illustrations and few words, this book aims to teach you the fundamentals of putting, whether you are a beginner or more experienced player who might need a refresher.

Happy Putting

The Team

Andrew Smith
Peter Syson
Paul Furnival

THE ANDREW'S BOOK COMPANY

Copyright © The Andrew's Book Company

The right of The Andrew's Book Company to be identified as the author of this work has been asserted in accordance with the Copyright, Designs and Patents Act 1988.

The R&A has given The Andrew's Book Company kind permission to print the rules in this book under the following conditions.

R&A Rules Limited and the United States Golf Association are the joint authors and owners of the copyright in the Rules of Golf (the "Rules"). All rights reserved to the copyright owners. This publication has not been approved or endorsed by R&A Rules Limited or the United States Golf Association.

First published July 2010 by
The Andrew's Book Company
156a Haxby Road, York YO31 8JN, United Kingdom
www.andrewsgolf.co.uk

All rights reserved. No part of this publication may be reproduced, stored in a retrieval system, or transmitted, in any form or by any means, electronic, mechanical, photocopying, recording or otherwise, without the prior permission of the publisher.

CIP catalogue records for this book are available from the British Library.

ISBN 978-0-9550248-1-8

Designed and produced by Rubber Band, York, UK

www.andrewsgolf.co.uk

©THE ANDREW'S BOOK COMPANY 2010

INTRODUCTION

It is often said that putting is a game within a game, this is very true.

Putting can make or break a player. One certainty is that there is never a great player who is not a great putter.

This book, devoted to putting, will guide you through the basics from the roll of the ball, how to hold a putter, stance, reading greens and choosing the correct putter to suit your style.

Our aim is to give you a consistent, repeatable putting stroke, which will inevitably reduce your scores.

In this book you will learn:

- The Roll
- Grip
- Posture
- Alignment
- Putting Stroke
- Swing Path
- Putters
- Reading the Green
- Prepare to Putt
- Long and Short Putts
- Practice
- The Modern Green
- Putting Rules

Andrew's

golf.co.uk

" A minimal error at the start leads to a wide divergence in the accuracy "

Chinese Proverb

CONTENTS

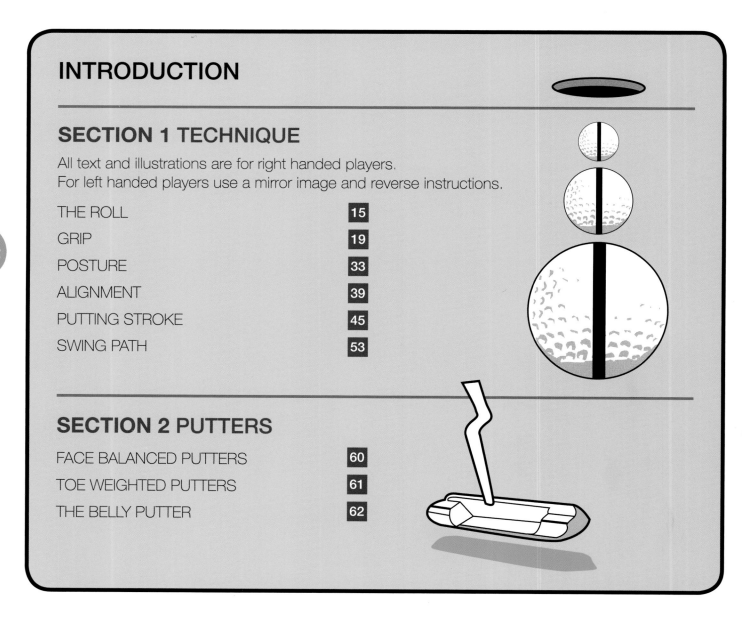

INTRODUCTION

SECTION 1 TECHNIQUE

All text and illustrations are for right handed players.
For left handed players use a mirror image and reverse instructions.

SECTION 2 PUTTERS

SECTION 3 LET'S PUTT

SECTION 4 THE GREEN

13

SECTION 5 THE RULES

TIPS, DID YOU KNOW & ETIQUETTE RUNNING THROUGHOUT THE BOOK.

TIP

Mark the ball with a line using a line me up ball marker.

DID YOU KNOW?

Hole size must be 4¼" or 108mm diameter and at least 4" or 101.6mm deep.

ETIQUETTE

Do not cast your shadow over your opponent's line.

Andrew's

golf.co.uk

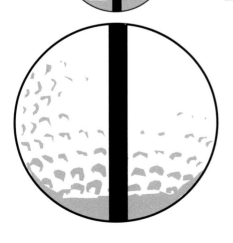

THE
ROLL

THE ROLL

...what does this mean?

Understanding this beforehand will help as we continue with technique

A perfect roll is a ball struck squarely towards the hole rolling top to tail without sidespin or wavering. Before we move onto technique it is important to grasp what we are trying to do with the ball.

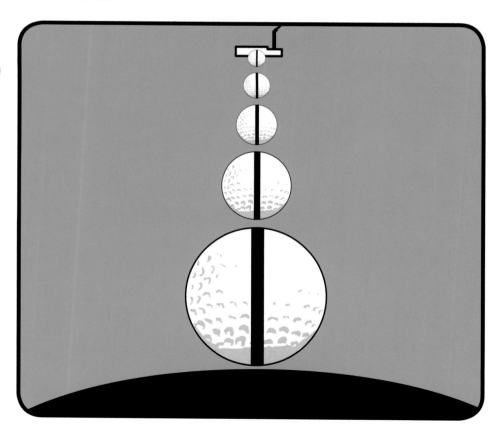

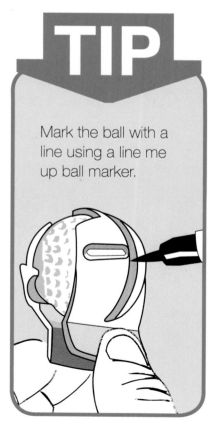

TIP

Mark the ball with a line using a line me up ball marker.

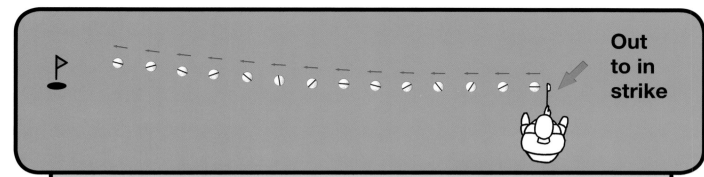

Out to in strike

Swing path out to in applying left to right spin. Generally the putt will be short.

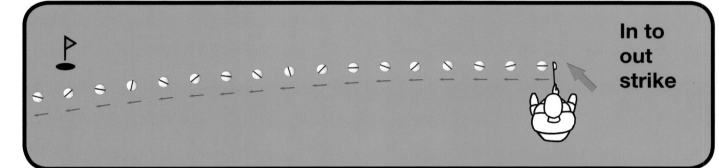

In to out strike

Swing path in to out applying right to left spin. Generally the putt will go long.

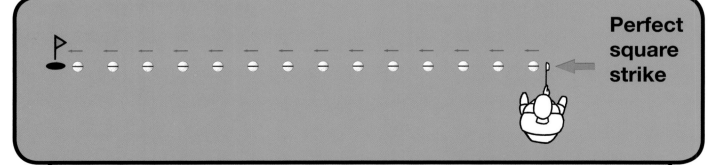

Perfect square strike

A lined up ball that is hit square will travel in a straight line and into the hole.

Andrew's

golf.co.uk

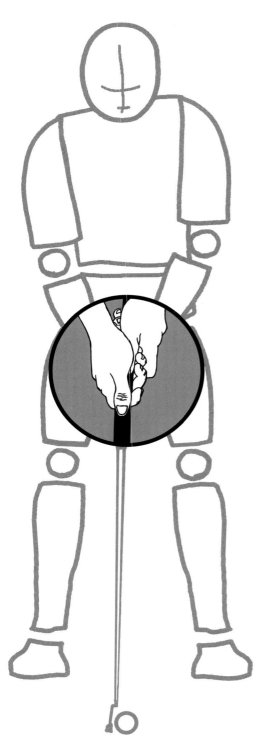

GRIP

CONVENTIONAL

GRIP ...conventional
overlap grip

The importance of a good grip is to maintain control of the putter head

The purpose of a good grip is to return the putter head square to the target.

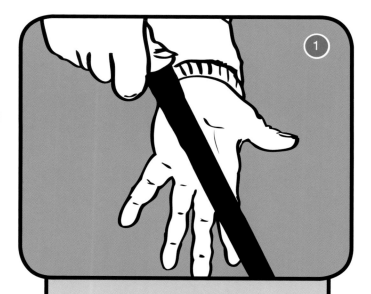

Pinch the top of the grip with the forefinger and thumb of your right hand and aim the face of the putter at the target.

Then place the putter grip along the lifeline on your left hand.

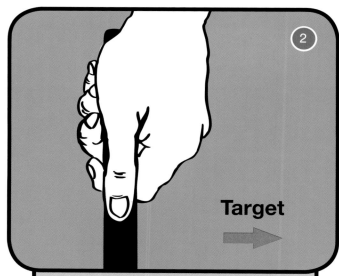

Target

Front view of your left hand clasped around grip with thumb resting on front flat side of grip. The back of your hand is facing the target.

③ Lift the left index finger free from the club to allow your right hand to fit snug underneath.

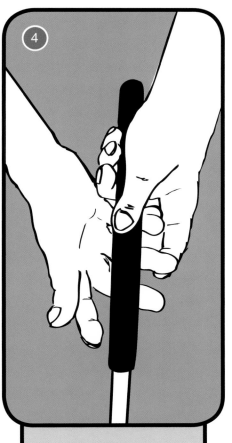

④ Place your right hand on the club below your left hand.

Rest the club in the joints of your fingers.

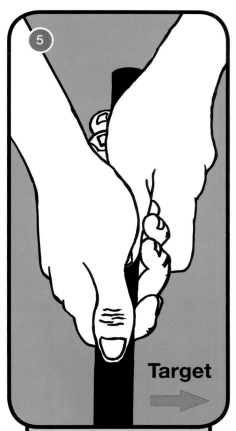

⑤ **Target**

Complete grip showing your left index finger resting on top of the fingers of your right hand. The back of your left hand should be facing the target.

This completes the conventional grip showing palms square to target and facing each other.

Andrew's

golf.co.uk

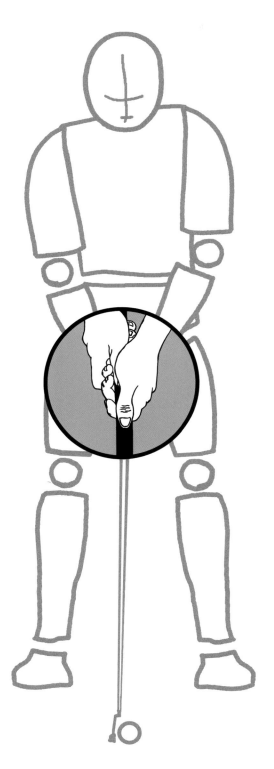

GRIP

UNCONVENTIONAL

GRIP ...unconventional
Left hand below right (cack handed)

The reason for this grip is to help maintain a straight left wrist.

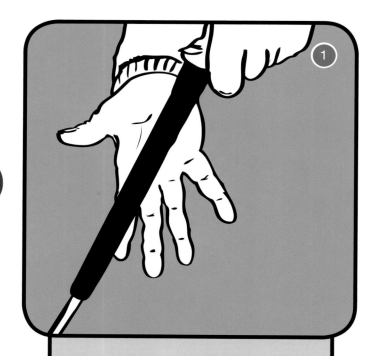

Pinch the top of the grip with the forefinger and thumb of your left hand and aim the face of the putter at the target.

Then place the putter grip along the lifeline on your right hand.

Target

Front view of your right hand clasped around grip with thumb resting on front flat side of grip. The palm of your hand is facing the target.

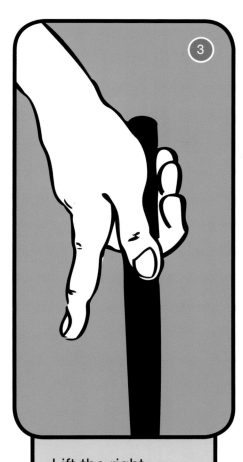

③

Lift the right index finger free from the club to allow your left hand to fit snug underneath.

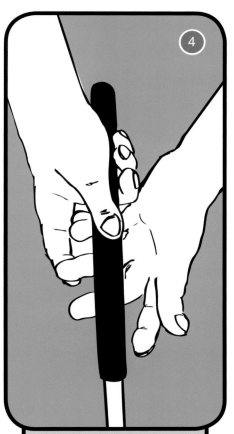

④

Place your left hand on the club below your right hand.

Rest the club in the joints of your fingers.

⑤

Target

Complete grip showing your right index finger resting on top of the fingers of your left hand. The back of your left hand should be facing the target.

This completes the unconventional grip showing palms square to target and facing each other.

Andrew's

golf.co.uk

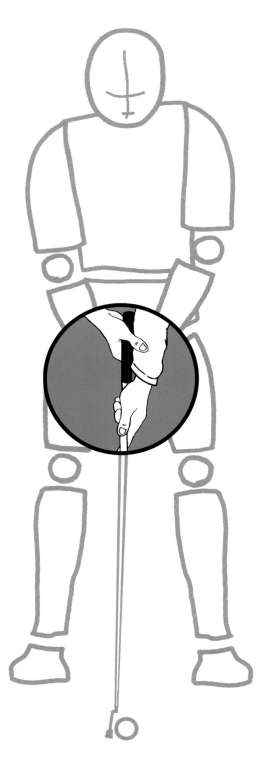

GRIP

SPLIT HAND

GRIP ...split hand

The split hand grip has evolved from players suffering from the yips, an involuntary twitch of the hand.

1

Rest your putter on the ground and hold the top of the grip in your right hand (this is to keep the club in position) and aim the face of the putter at the target.

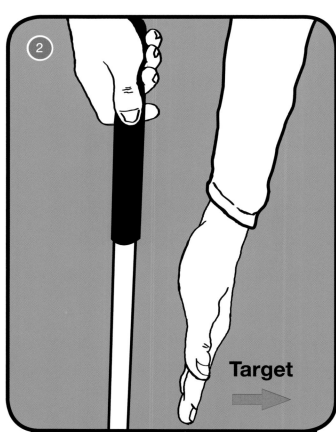

2

Target

Whilst holding the putter in your right hand stretch out left hand, making sure the back of your left hand is facing towards the target.

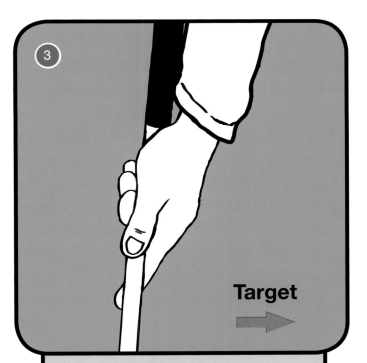

Target

Bring your left hand towards the putter shaft and wrap your hand around the shaft. Remove your right hand and ensure the shaft is along your forearm, with the back of your hand facing the target.

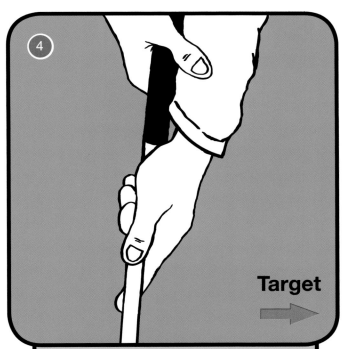

Target

Grasp your forearm over the putter shaft with your right hand. The back of your hand should be facing the target.

GRIP ...how much pressure?

Lightly does it

Gripping your club with the wrong amount of pressure can effect the speed at which you want the ball to travel. It is important to keep your grip pressure constant throughout the putting stroke.

How Tight?

- is letting your putter rest in your hand without pressure
- is gripping as tight as you can
- is just right

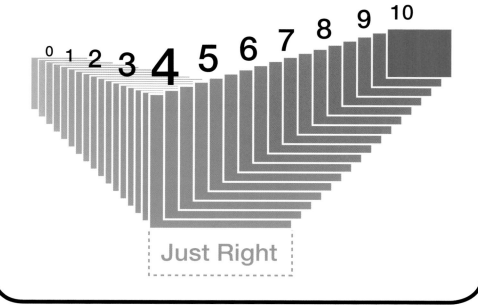

0 1 2 3 **4** 5 6 7 8 9 10

Just Right

TIP

Check the condition of your putter handle, as a worn or dirty handle will cause you to grip the club too tightly.

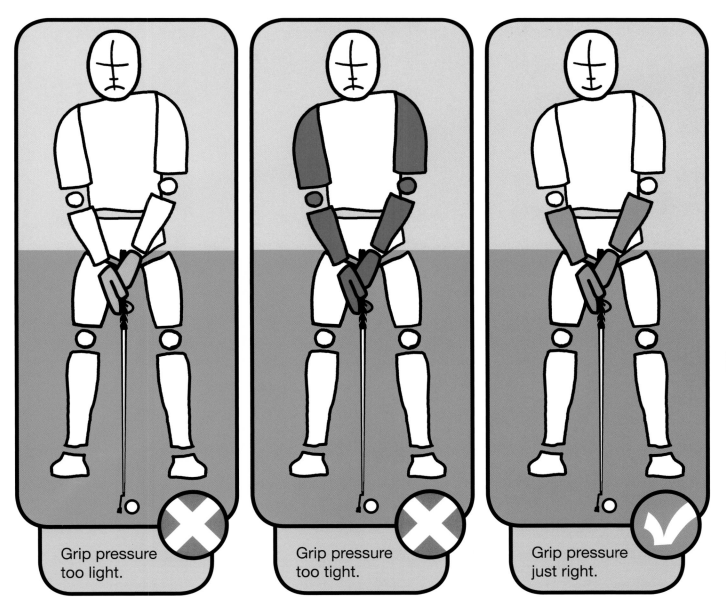

Grip pressure
too light.

Grip pressure
too tight.

Grip pressure
just right.

DID YOU KNOW? Hole size must be 4¼" or 108mm diameter and at least 4" or 101.6mm deep.

Andrew's

golf.co.uk

POSTURE

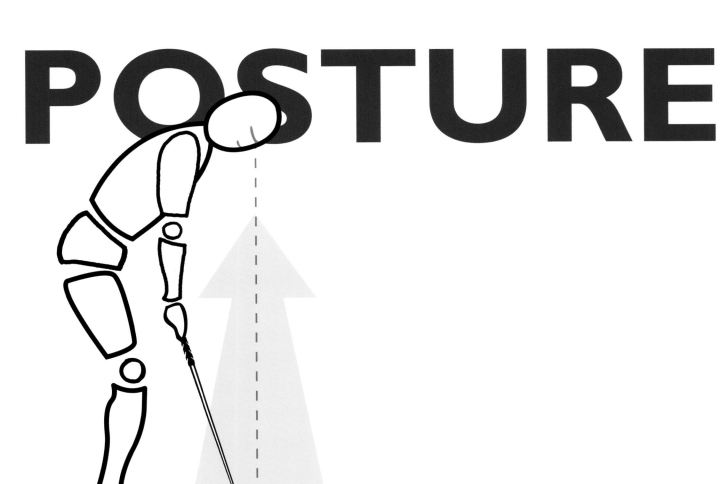

POSTURE

...perfect preparation

Good posture sets your eyes above the ball

Most people would fire a gun by looking directly down the barrel to the target.

Keep your eyes directly over the ball so that they are directly in line with the target.

How to achieve correct posture

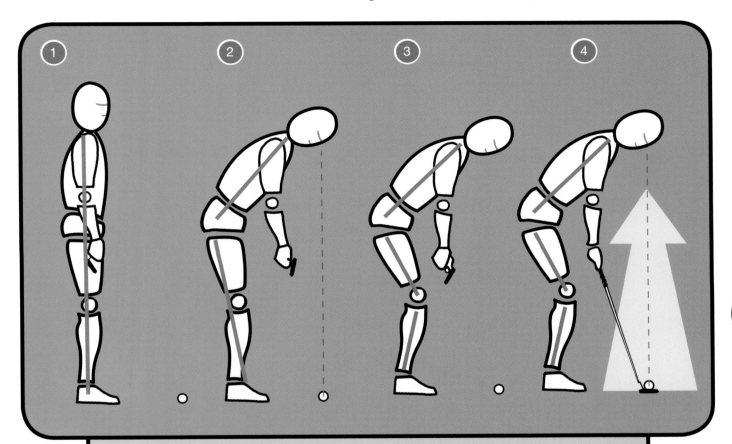

1. Stand up straight, parallel to your intended line of putt.

2. Keeping back straight, bend over until your eyes are over the ball. Let your arms fall forward.

3. Flex your knees, bring arms together.

4. Now adopt your grip of the putter and place the putter head behind the ball. We are now ready to make a putting stroke.

POSTURE

...eyes over the ball

Here is a simple drill to help

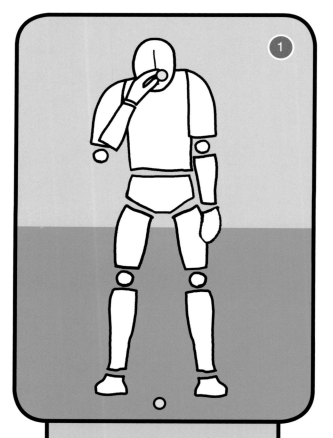

Place a ball on the ground. Stand as normal and hold a ball to your left eye.

Try position yourself so that the ball in your hand is over the ball on the ground.

How to achieve correct posture.

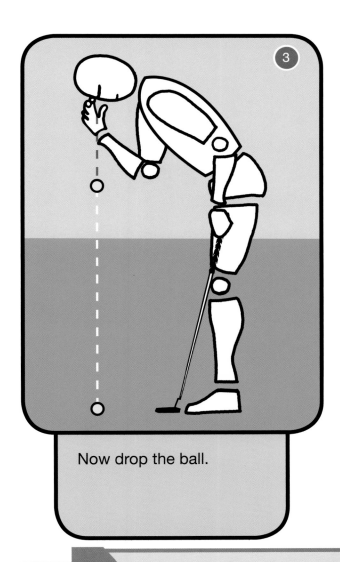

3

Now drop the ball.

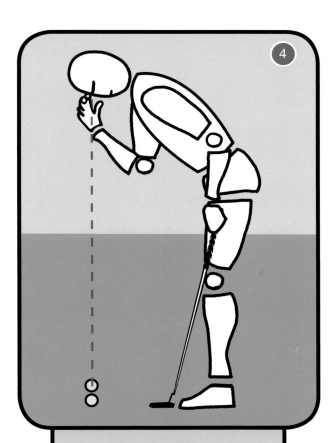

4

If your eyes are in the correct position the dropped ball will land on the ball on the ground.

DID YOU KNOW?

A stimpmeter is a device for measuring the speed of the greens. A ball is placed at one end of the stimpmeter and held in position by a notch. The stimpmeter is then raised until the ball rolls off it and onto the green. How far the ball rolls is the stimpmeter reading.

Andrew's

golf.co.uk

ALIGNMENT

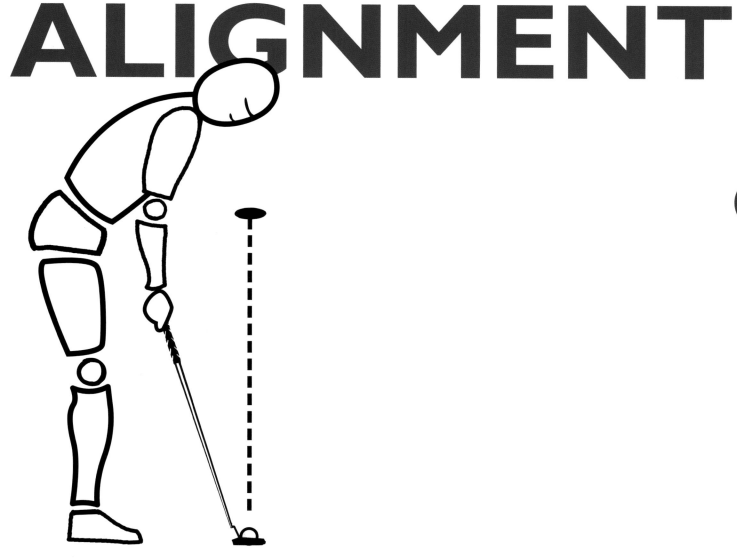

ALIGNMENT

...choose your target

Every putt is straight. The lie of the land dictates the amount of brake (movement sideways) the ball will take on its way to the hole.

For flat putts, the hole will be your target.

For long putts, or across a slope, you can use a **natural** mark on the green as the target. This could be a blemish on the green or similar.

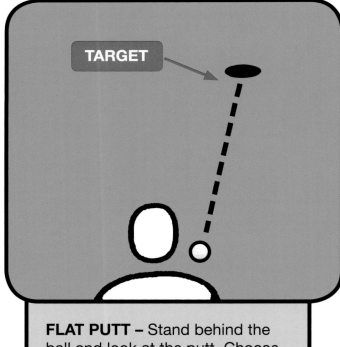

FLAT PUTT – Stand behind the ball and look at the putt. Choose your target and run your eyes back to the ball.

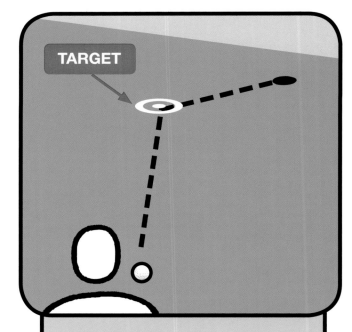

SLOPING PUTT – Stand behind the ball and choose your target. This is the point at which the ball will move sideways following the contours of the green.

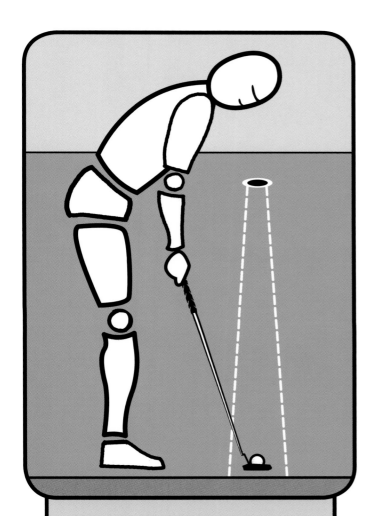

Your target on a straight putt on a flat surface is the hole.

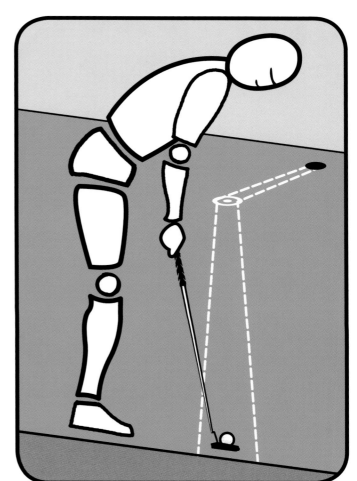

Your target on a putt across a slope that has a break in it, is the point at which the ball will move sideways.

ETIQUETTE

When another player has marked his ball, be careful not to stand on his line of putt.

ALIGNMENT

...focus your eyes on the line

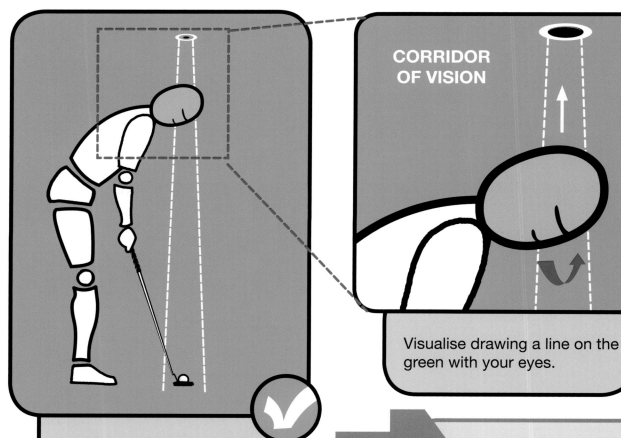

CORRIDOR OF VISION

Visualise drawing a line on the green with your eyes.

Only have eyes for the line. It is important that you twist your head so that your eyes will run along the line.

DID YOU KNOW?

A ball is holed when it is at rest within the circumference of the hole and all of it is below the level of the lip of the hole.

Avoid lifting your head to look at the line

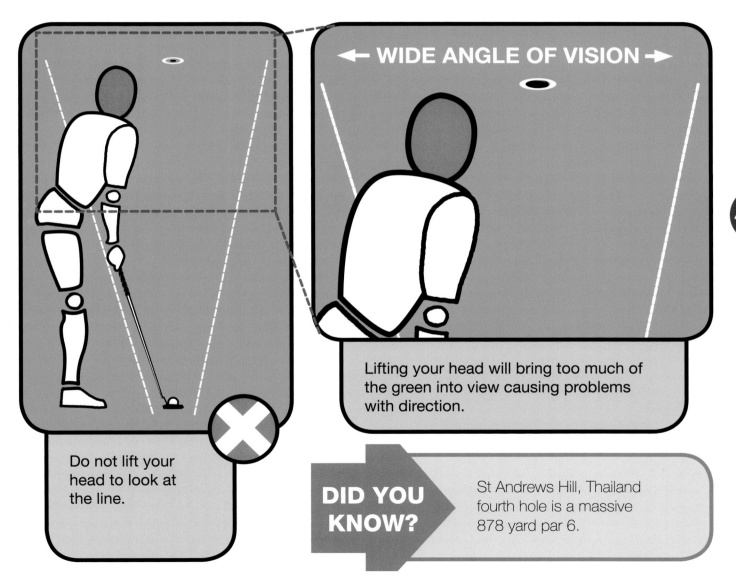

WIDE ANGLE OF VISION

Lifting your head will bring too much of the green into view causing problems with direction.

Do not lift your head to look at the line.

DID YOU KNOW? St Andrews Hill, Thailand fourth hole is a massive 878 yard par 6.

43

Andrew's

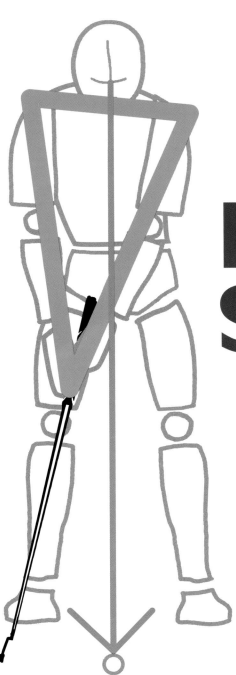

PUTTING STROKE

PUTTING STROKE

...short and medium putts

Keep it simple

The less moving parts in a putting stroke the easier it is to return the putter to its starting point.

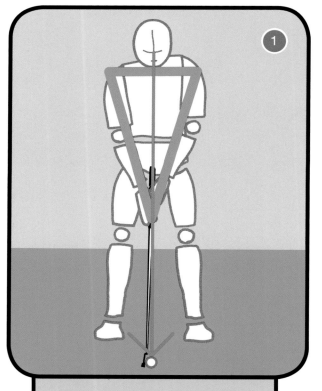

Avoid tension, relax and apply the correct grip pressure. Eyes positioned over the ball.

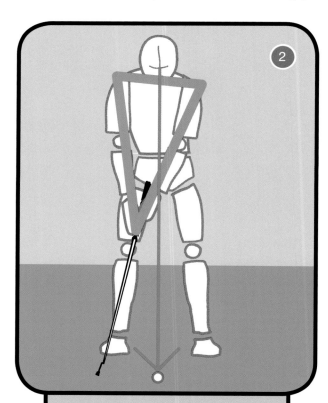

Try to swing the putter like a pendulum from your shoulders, swing smoothly.

In 1989 Nick Faldo sank a 100' putt birdie on the 2nd at Augusta.

The longest putt holed to date.

Do not cast your shadow over your opponent's line.

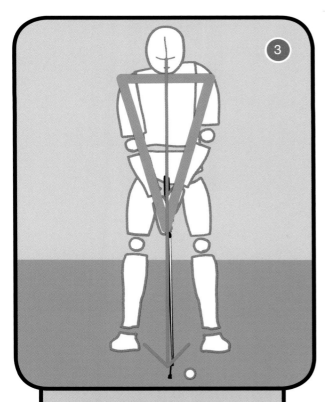

Accelerate through the ball at impact.

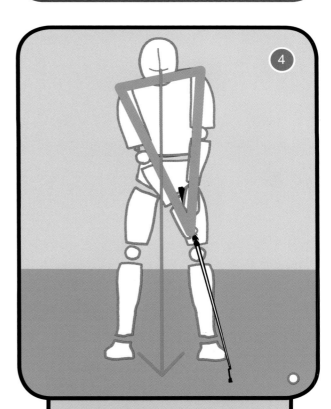

Your through swing should be longer than your back swing. Eyes still looking at the ground.

PUTTING STROKE

...long putts

Still keep it simple

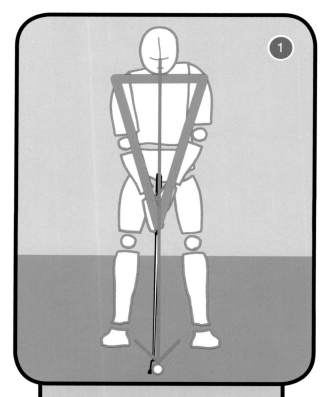

Avoid tension, relax and apply the correct grip pressure. Eyes positioned over the ball.

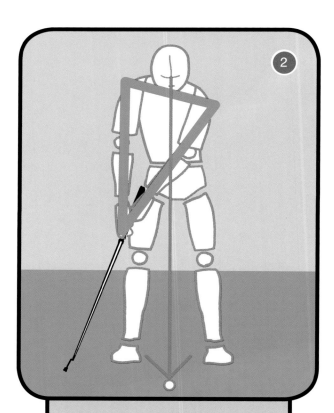

Keep the connection between your arms and the body throughout the stroke. There should be no movement from the waist down.

DID YOU KNOW?

Most players take their glove off whilst putting, the reason is to get a better feel of the putter and maintain equal pressure on both hands.

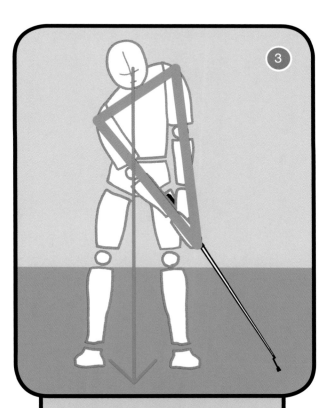

The putter has accelerated through impact. Eyes looking at the ground.

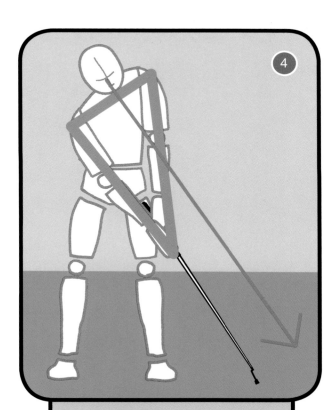

Only after the ball has travelled 3 yards should you tilt your head to watch the ball travelling towards the hole.

PUTTING STROKE

...eliminate wrist action

Too much wrist action will result in an inconsistent ball strike and poor direction

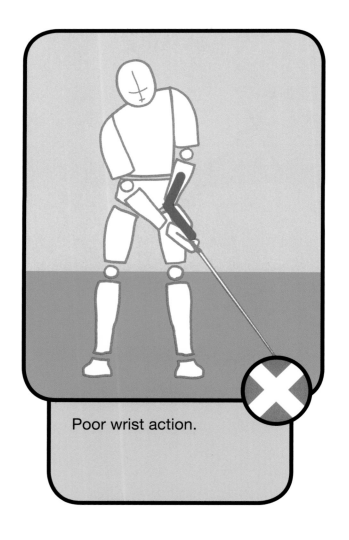

Poor wrist action.

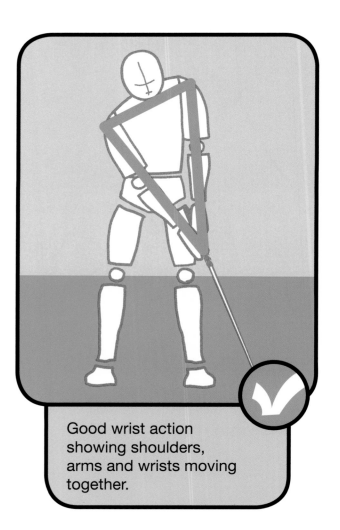

Good wrist action showing shoulders, arms and wrists moving together.

Exercises to help eliminate wrist action

Slip a pen behind your watch and practice your stroke. This will firm up your left wrist.

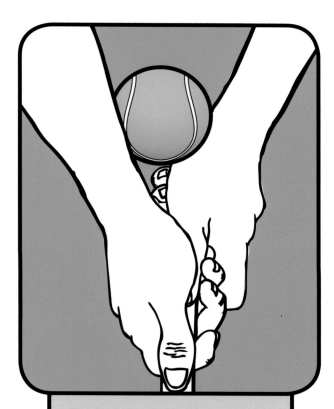

Place a tennis ball between wrists and practice your stroke.

DID YOU KNOW?

To mark the position of your ball on the green and subsequently lift it, you are recommended to use a ball-marker or small coin. However, you are allowed to use something else like a tee or the putter head.

Andrew's

golf.co.uk

SWING PATH

SWING PATH

...the important ingredient in returning the putter face back to its starting position

How to take the putter back and
through when hitting the ball

There are three types of swing path.

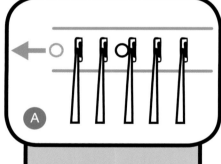

A

Straight back to
square to straight
through.

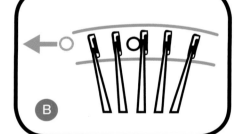

B

Back inside the line
to square through to
inside the line.

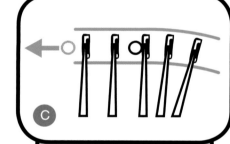

C

Back inside the line
to square to straight
through.

ETIQUETTE

When playing on or near the putting green players should
leave their bags or carts in a position so they can pick
them up on their way to the next tee.

Straight back to square to straight through

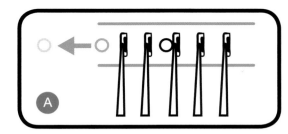

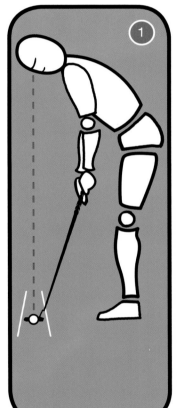

1 Aim your putter head at the target and adopt the correct stance.

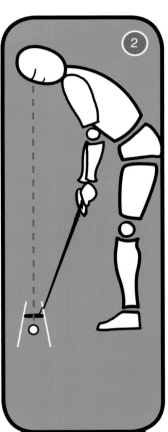

2 Swing your putter back in a straight line, eyes still looking at the ball.

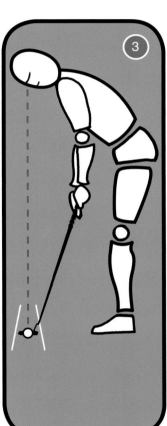

3 At impact your eyes should still be looking at the ball.

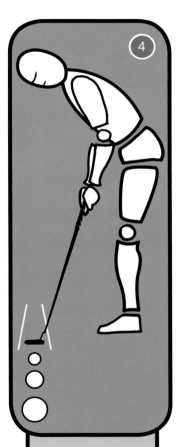

4 Swing straight through keeping the putter face square to the target.

Back inside the line to square through to inside the line

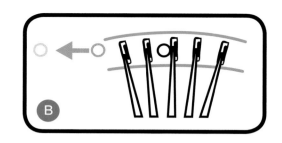

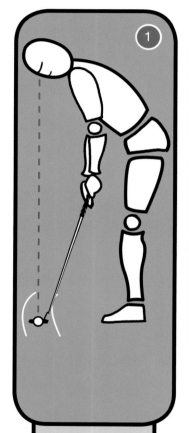

1 Aim your putter head at the target and adopt the correct stance.

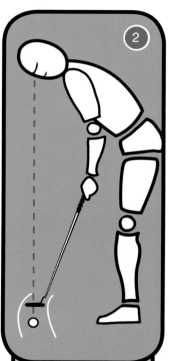

2 Swing your putter back inside the line, eyes still looking at the ball. You will need a slight turn of the shoulders.

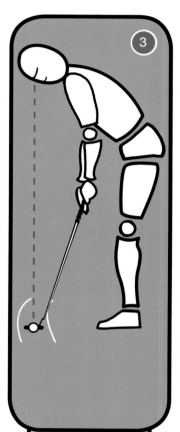

3 At impact your eyes should still be looking at the ball.

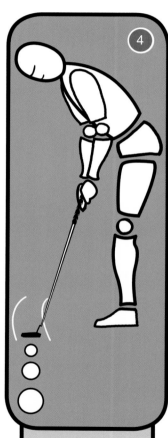

4 Swing your putter through just inside the line allowing your shoulders to turn slightly.

Back inside the line to square to straight through

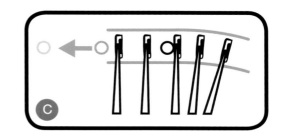

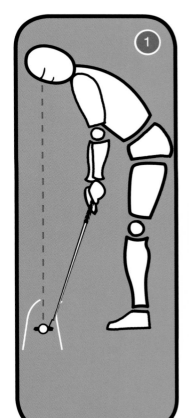

1. Aim your putter head at the target and adopt the correct stance.

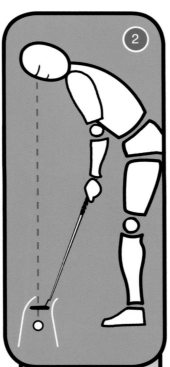

2. Swing your putter back inside the line, eyes still looking at the ball. You will need a slight turn of the shoulders.

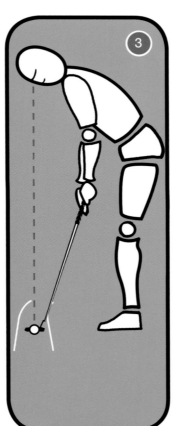

3. At impact your eyes should still be looking at the ball.

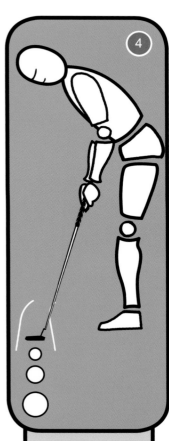

4. Swing straight through keeping the putter face square to the target.

Andrew's

golf.co.uk

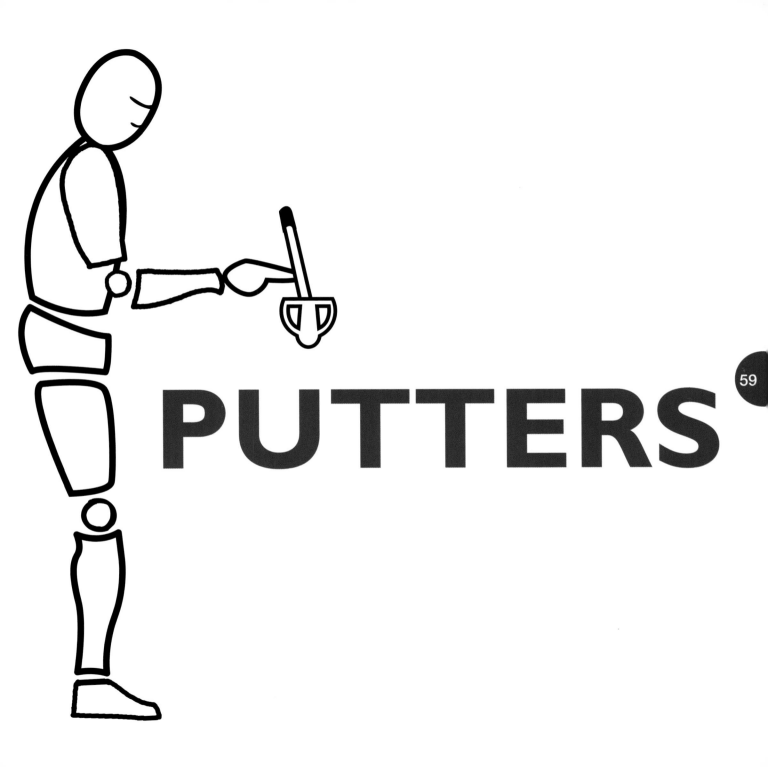

PUTTERS

59

PUTTERS

...which putter is right for me?

A basic guide to putters and their uses

Putters come in different lengths.

There are also two types of putter – face balanced putters and toe weighted putters. Try them and choose the one that suits you the best.

Putter lengths

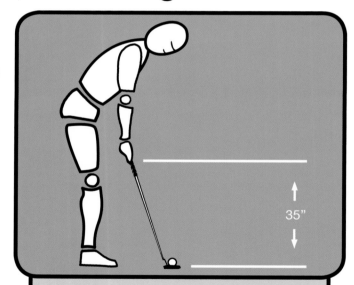

35"

Most commonly 35" also 33" to 34". Most people would buy a putter to suit their height. However, a tall person may use a short putter to crouch over the ball. Speak to your supplier or golf coach.

Face balanced putter

Heel

Toe

A face balanced putter lies horizontal when balanced in your hand.

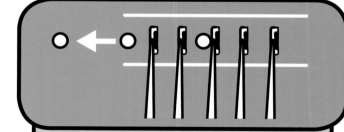

A face balanced putter is best suited to a straight back and straight through putting action.

Toe weighted putters

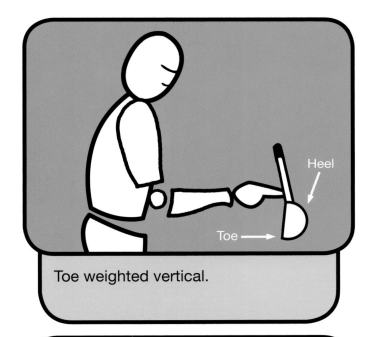

Toe weighted vertical.

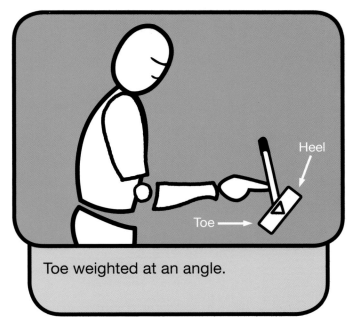

Toe weighted at an angle.

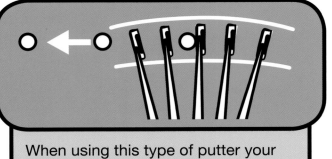

When using this type of putter your stroke should be back inside the line to square to back inside the line.

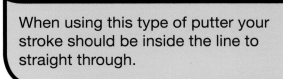

When using this type of putter your stroke should be inside the line to straight through.

THE BELLY PUTTER

The objective is to help eliminate wrist action

Longer than normal putter measuring 44"/48". The idea is to anchor the putter in your belly.

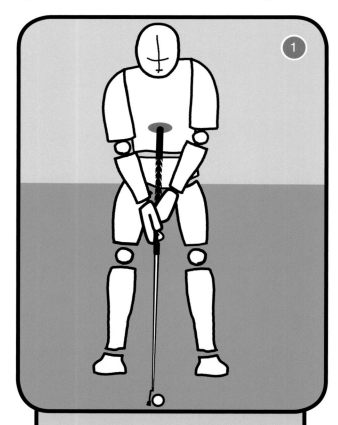

Anchor the bottom end of the putter against your stomach and adopt your normal grip.

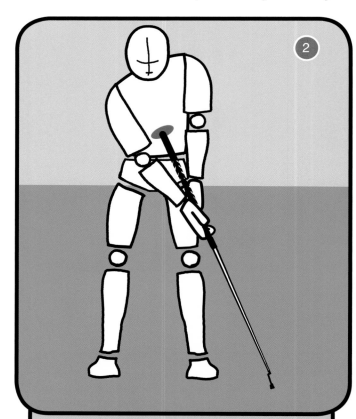

Keep the butt end firmly in your stomach and the putter will swing like a pendulum.

Your stomach will become an anchorpoint, so that you can produce a consistent accelerating stroke.

Alternative grip using the belly putter

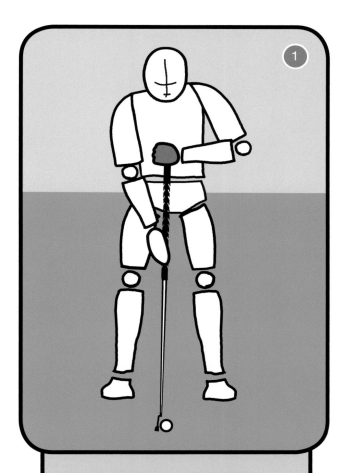

An alternative way of using the belly putter is to hold the butt end of the putter in your stomach.

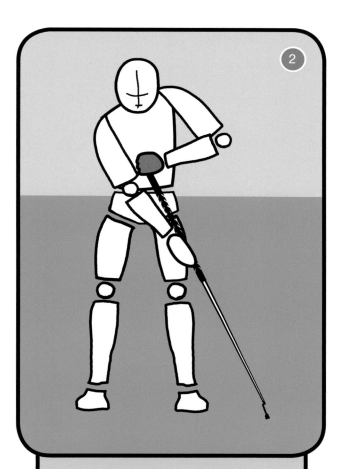

Your right hand will guide the putter and produce power.

Andrew's

golf.co.uk

READING THE GREEN

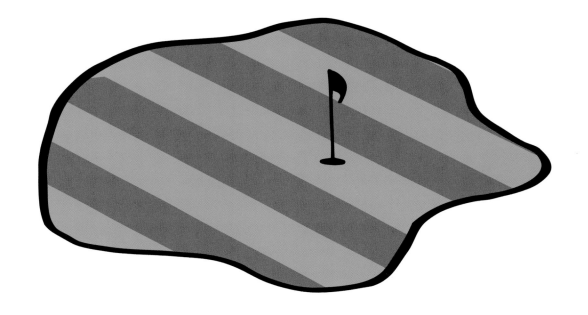

READING THE GREEN

...be aware of the conditions

Weather conditions play a huge part in the speed and direction of a putt. As you approach the green think about how the weather will affect the roll of your ball.

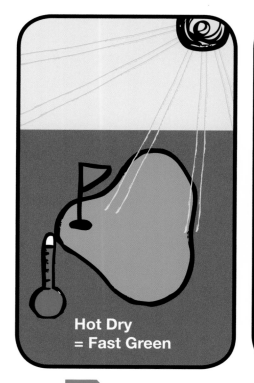

Hot Dry = Fast Green

Cold and Wet = Slow Green

Windy Day

The wind will affect the speed of the ball = Slow into wind = Fast down wind

Wind will also blow the ball off line

TIP Visit the practice green. The practice green should be cut the same as the greens on the course, therefore running at the same speed.

Reading the grain of the green

The putting green will be cut every day, usually early on a morning. The grass will be cut in different directions. The direction the grass is cut will determine the lay of the grass. This is called 'the grain'.

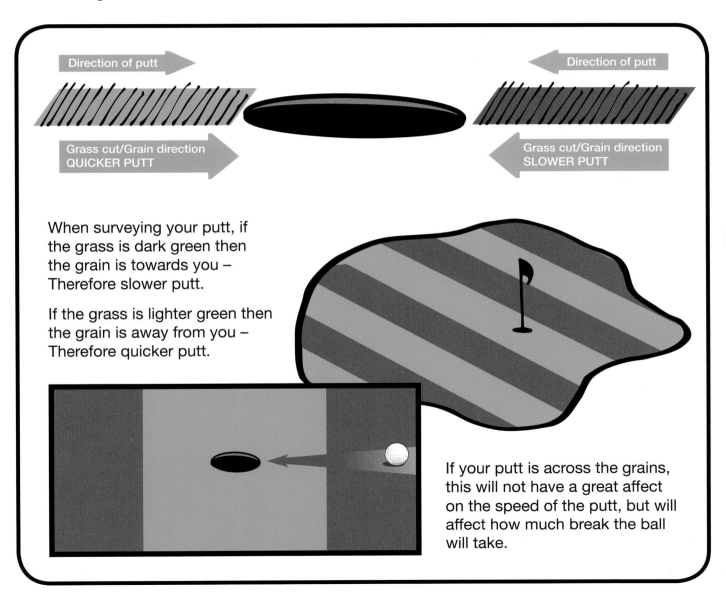

Direction of putt

Direction of putt

Grass cut/Grain direction
QUICKER PUTT

Grass cut/Grain direction
SLOWER PUTT

When surveying your putt, if the grass is dark green then the grain is towards you – Therefore slower putt.

If the grass is lighter green then the grain is away from you – Therefore quicker putt.

If your putt is across the grains, this will not have a great affect on the speed of the putt, but will affect how much break the ball will take.

Andrew's

golf.co.uk

PREPARE TO
PUTT

PREPARE TO PUTT

...repair, pick up and clean

Good habits before putting

Once on the green, and before you study your putt, there are essential tasks to perform.

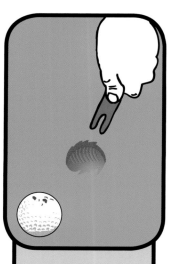

A pitchmark is an indentation caused when the ball lands on the green. Use a pitchmark repair fork and lift out the pitchmark.

Once your ball is on the putting surface you are allowed to mark the ball, pick up and clean.

Clean your ball for a perfect roll.

Clean your putter face for perfect contact. Water and grit can alter the clubface to ball contact.

Look for loose impediments that can be removed.

Using the mark on the ball to get your line

Target

After cleaning your ball replace with line pointing at the target.

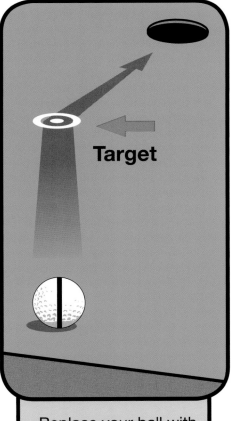

Target

Replace your ball with the line facing your interim target.

DID YOU KNOW?

The average score amongst club golfers in America was reportedly 98.6.

TIP

When you have chosen your line look for a mark on the green about 3 feet ahead of your ball and try to putt your ball over this mark.

Andrew's

golf.co.uk

PUTTING
THE LONG
AND SHORT
OF IT

THE LONG PUTT

...across a slope

Get the picture – survey the putt from all angles

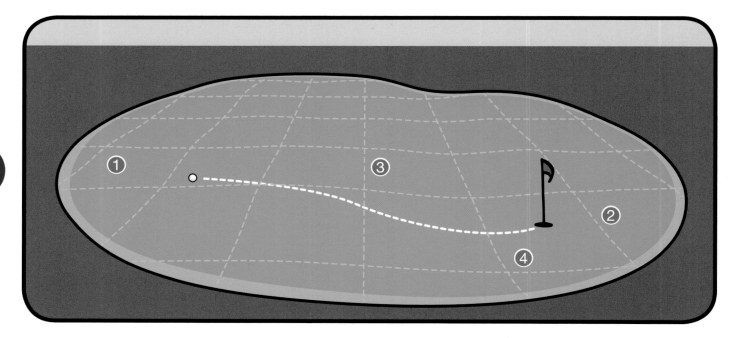

1. To assess the slope look at the putt from behind the ball.

2. Look at the putt from behind the hole and leave the flag in. This will help you see the slope.

3. Look at the putt from the side to assess the slope.

4. Look at the final 2 yards and look inside the hole – this will give you a little more information about the grain.

DID YOU KNOW?

You may adjust the flagstick so that it is centered, you may not however adjust it so that it is leaning away from you.

Information is the key

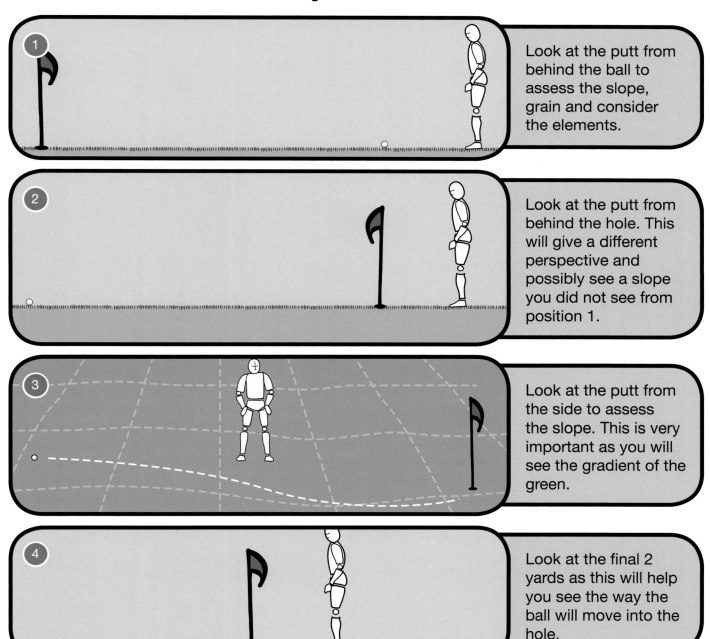

1. Look at the putt from behind the ball to assess the slope, grain and consider the elements.

2. Look at the putt from behind the hole. This will give a different perspective and possibly see a slope you did not see from position 1.

3. Look at the putt from the side to assess the slope. This is very important as you will see the gradient of the green.

4. Look at the final 2 yards as this will help you see the way the ball will move into the hole.

THE SHORT PUTT

...across a slope

3 ways to play the same putt

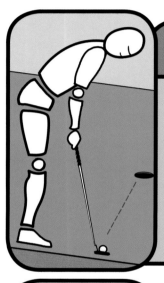

1 FIRM PUTT – COURAGE

Taking the brake out.

You may opt to hit the putt firmly – this will mean the ball will not be affected by the slope.

ADVANTAGE – Will not be affected by slope/spike marks/grain. You will only have to aim straight.

DISADVANTAGE – If you miss the hole, the ball may shoot past the hole and be further away than when you started.

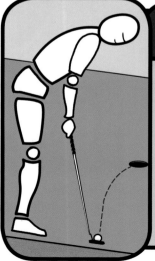

2 MEDIUM PUTT – HEDGING YOUR BET

Taking part of the brake out.

This will need to be played at medium pace allowing for the slope of the green to move sideways.

ADVANTAGE – If you miss the putt it should still be reasonably close.

DISADVANTAGE – Slope and spike marks will come into play.

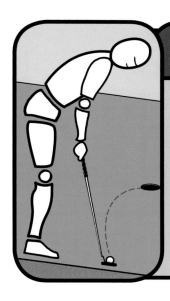

SOFT PUTT – GUARANTEED 2 PUTTS

Playing the whole brake.

This putt will be played softly allowing the slope to move the ball towards the hole.

ADVANTAGE – Easier to guarantee 2 putts.

DISADVANTAGE – By playing the ball softly you will have to judge the slope correctly, also a soft putt will be more susceptible to moving off line by hitting spike marks. The grain will have more influence on the ball at a slow pace.

THE SHORT PUTT

...on a flat green

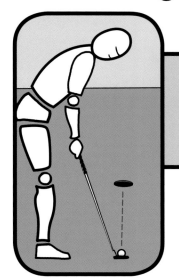

This is often thought to be an easy putt but mistakes can be made through carelessness. Aim at the centre of the hole and stroke the ball in with a smooth action, hit the ball firm enough so that the ball will hit the back of the hole.

ETIQUETTE

Try not to stand with your feet too close to the hole when picking your ball out. This could damage the edge of the hole.

Andrew's

golf.co.uk

PRACTICE

PRACTICE

...inside

It has been known for top golfers to practice their putting stroke whilst standing on their snooker table at home. Whilst we may not all have a snooker table, it does show you can, with imagination, practice away from the course.

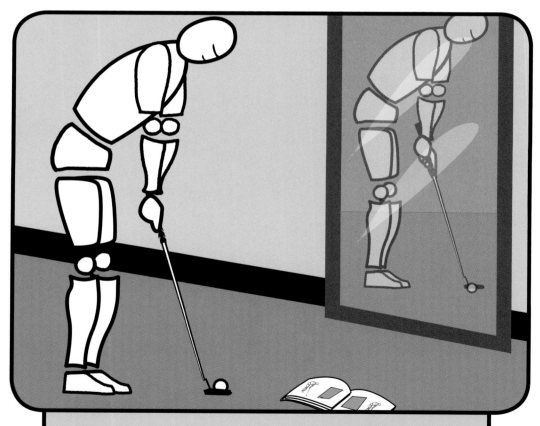

Place the book on the floor and stand in front of a mirror to check your position and stroke.

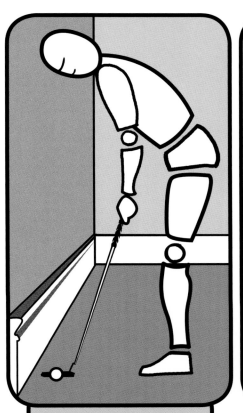

Practice your strokes against the skirting board to make sure you're lined up square and are taking your club back and forth correctly.

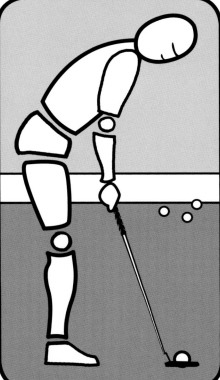

Practice distance control towards the skirting board. Get as close as possible without touching.

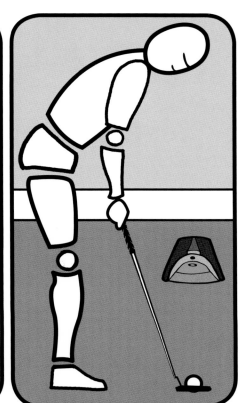

An indoor putting machine is an inexpensive way to practice your stroke at home.

TIP Put a putting machine on your Christmas or birthday present list.

PRACTICE

...outside

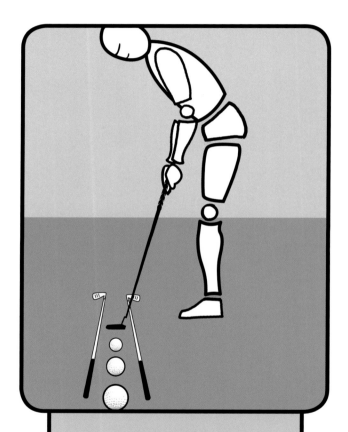

Clubs on Ground

Rest 2 clubs on the green and practice your stroke to ensure you are swinging your putter through in a straight line.

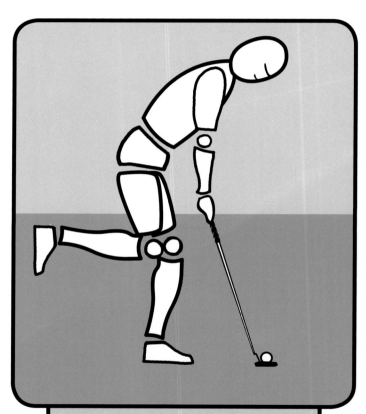

Stand on One Leg

Practice standing on one leg to improve your balance and to help maintain a steady head.

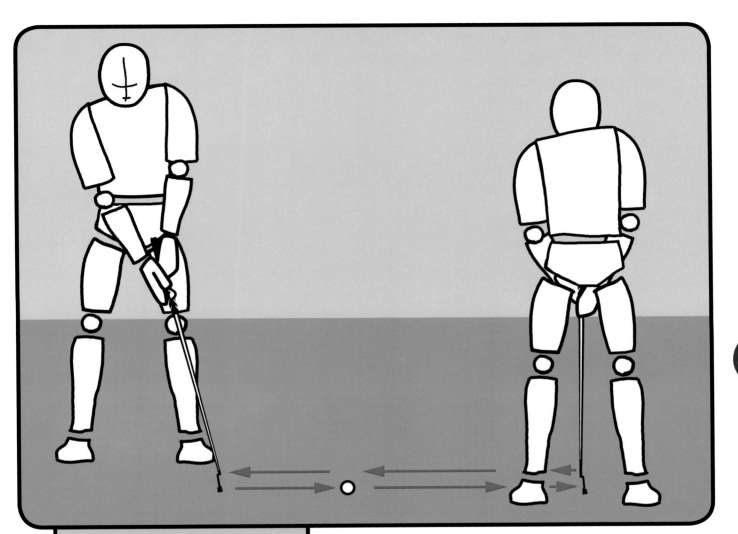

Penalty Shoot Out

Partners Game.
Try to hit your partner's putter head – each time you succeed it's a goal. Have 5 goes each to find the winner.

TIP Practice putting with your eyes closed.

PRACTICE OUTSIDE

...ball speed

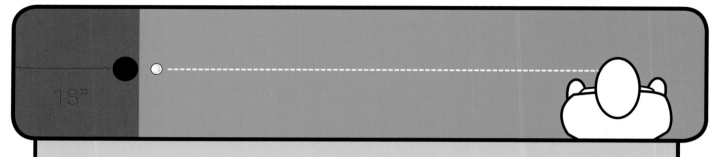

Always try to hit the ball firm enough so that if you miss the hole the ball will travel **18" past the hole.** The reason is that a ball travelling at this speed is more likely to hold its line and not be affected by spike marks and indentations on the green.

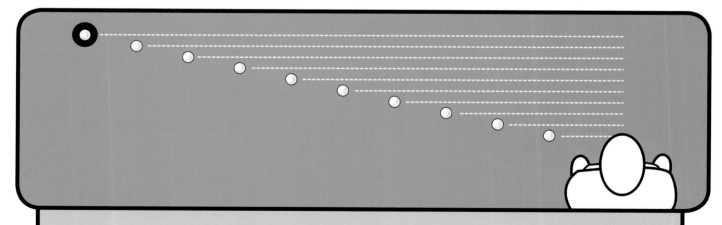

Start with 10 balls, hit the first ball a short distance then the next ball a little further and so on. Try and get as many balls as possible between you and the hole. As soon as one ball goes into the hole or beyond the game is over.

Practice from all sides of the hole

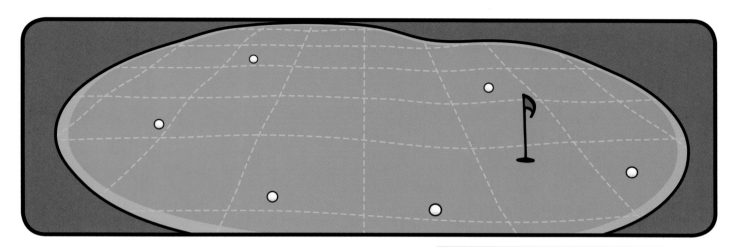

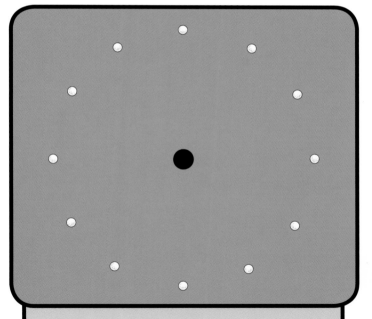

Practice around the clock to see how many balls you can hole out of twelve.

TIP

Make the Hole Smaller

Place tee pegs on both sides of the hole, this will block the hole leaving a small gap. When you go back to putting at a normal size hole it should seem a lot larger than normal.

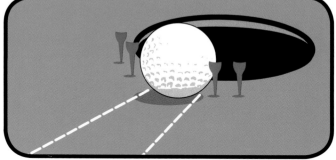

Andrew's

golf.co.uk

THE MODERN GREEN

THE MODERN GREEN

- To create more interest, the green is often undulating.
- The apron is a band of grass around a putting green where the grass is slightly longer.
- You may NOT mark your ball on the apron.

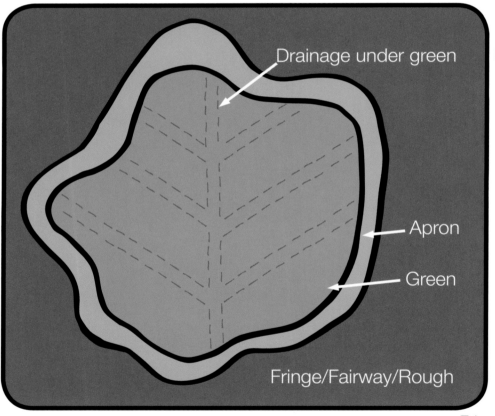

Drainage under green

Apron

Green

Fringe/Fairway/Rough

DID YOU KNOW?

Reasearch was being carried out on soils for greens and construction as early as 1956 by Dr O. R. Lunt from the University of California.

Green
cut short

Apron
cut approx ⅛" (3mm)

Fringe/Fairway/Rough
cut approx 1" (25mm)

Looking through a green showing the drainage pipes

The modern green is designed to be free draining and requires constant water via an efficient sprinkler system.

Green

Top Soil 12" (300mm)

Coarse Sand 1" (25mm)

Pea Gravel 4" (100mm)

Drainage Pipe

Native Soil

Andrew's

golf.co.uk

PUTTING RULES

RULE 7: Practice

7-1 Before or Between Rounds (a) Match Play

On any day of a match play competition, a player may practise on the competition course before a round.

7-1 Before or Between Rounds (b) Stroke Play

Before a round or play-off on any day of a stroke play competition, a competitor must not practise on the competition course or test the surface of any putting green on the course by rolling a ball or roughening or scraping the surface.

When two or more rounds of a stroke play competition are to be played over consecutive days, a competitor must not practise between those rounds on any competition course remaining to be played, or test the surface of any putting green on such course by rolling a ball or roughening or scraping the surface.

7-2 During Round

A player must not make a practice stroke during play of a hole.

Between the play of two holes a player must not make a practice stroke, except that he may practise putting or chipping on or near:

a. the putting green of the hole last played;

b. any practice putting green, or

c. the teeing ground of the next hole to be played in the round,

provided a practice stroke is not made from a hazard and does not unduly delay play (Rule 6-7).

Strokes made in continuing the play of a hole, the result of which has been decided, are not practice strokes.

Exception

When play has been suspended by the Committee, a player may, prior to resumption of play, practise (a) as provided in this Rule, (b) anywhere other than on the competition course and (c) as otherwise permitted by the Committee.

Penalty for Breach of Rule 7-2:

Match play – Loss of hole; Stroke play – Two strokes. In the event of a breach between the play of two holes, the penalty applies to the next hole.

Exception

Practice putting or chipping on or near the first teeing ground before starting a round or play-off is permitted.

Penalty for Breach of Rule 7-1b:

Disqualification

Practice During a Round

Practice putting on or near the tee of the next hole to be played is permitted as long as play is not delayed.

NOTE 1

A practice swing is not a practice stroke and may be taken at any place, provided the player does not breach the Rules.

NOTE 2

The Committee may, in the conditions of a competition (Rule 33-1), prohibit:

a. practice on or near the putting green of the hole last played, and

b. rolling a ball on the putting green of the hole last played.

RULE 8:
Advice; Indicating Line of Play

8-2 Indicating Line of Play (a) Other Than on Putting Green

Except on the putting green, a player may have the line of play indicated to him by anyone, but no one may be positioned by the player on or close to the line or an extension of the line beyond the hole while the stroke is being made. Any mark placed by the player or with his knowledge to indicate the line must be removed before the stroke is made.

8-2 Indicating Line of Play (b) On the Putting Green

When the player's ball is on the putting green, the player, his partner or either of their caddies may, before but not during the stroke, point out a line for putting, but in so doing the putting green must not be touched. A mark must not be placed anywhere to indicate a line for putting.

Exception

Flagstick attended or held up – see Rule 17-1.

Penalty for Breach of Rule:

Match play – Loss of hole;
Stroke play – Two strokes.

NOTE The Committee may, in the conditions of a team competition (Rule 33-1), permit each team to appoint one person who may give advice (including pointing out a line for putting) to members of that team. The Committee may establish conditions relating to the appointment and permitted conduct of that person, who must be identified to the Committee before giving advice.

RULE 14:
Striking the Ball

14-1 Ball to be Fairly Struck At

The ball must be fairly struck at with the head of the club and must not be pushed, scraped or spooned.

14-2 Assistance

In making a stroke, a player must not:

a.   accept physical assistance or protection from the elements; or

b.   allow his caddie, his partner or his partner's caddie to position himself on or close to an extension of the line of play or the line of putt behind the ball.

RULE 16:
The Putting Green

16 Definition - The Putting Green

The putting green is all ground of the hole being played which is specially prepared for putting or otherwise defined as such by the Committee. A ball is on the putting green when any part of it touches the putting green.

The line of putt is the line which the player wishes his ball to take after a stroke on the putting green. Except with respect to Rule 16-1e, the line of putt includes a reasonable distance on either side of the intended line. The line of putt does not extend beyond the hole.

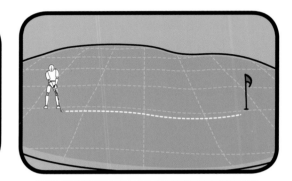

16-1 General (a) Touching Line of Putt

The line of putt must not be touched except:

(i) the player may remove loose impediments, provided he does not press anything down;

(ii) the player may place the club in front of the ball when addressing it, provided he does not press anything down;

(iii) in measuring – Rule 18-6;

(iv) in lifting or replacing the ball – Rule 16-1b;

(v) in pressing down a ball-marker;

(vi) in repairing old hole plugs or ball marks on the putting green – Rule 16-1c; and

(vii) in removing movable obstructions – Rule 24-1.

(Indicating line for putting on putting green – see Rule 8-2b).

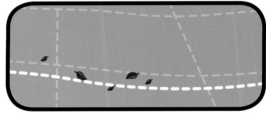

Penalty for Breach of Rule 16-1:

Match play – Loss of hole;
Stroke play – Two strokes.

16-1 General (b) Lifting Ball

A ball on the putting green may be lifted and, if desired, cleaned. The position of the ball must be marked before it is lifted and the ball must be replaced (see Rule 20-1).

16-1 General (c) Repair of Hole Plugs, Ball Marks and Other Damage

The player may repair an old hole plug or damage to the putting green caused by the impact of a ball, whether or not the player's ball lies on the putting green. If a ball or ball-marker is accidentally moved in the process of repair, the ball or ball-marker shall be replaced, without penalty. Any other damage to the putting green shall not be repaired if it might assist the player in his subsequent play of the hole.

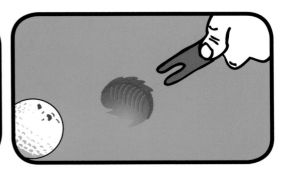

16-1 General (d) Testing Surface

During the stipulated round, a player must not test the surface of any putting green by rolling a ball or roughening or scraping the surface.

16-1 General (e) Standing Astride or On Line of Putt

The player must not make a stroke on the putting green from a stance astride, or with either foot touching, the line of putt or an extension of that line behind the ball.

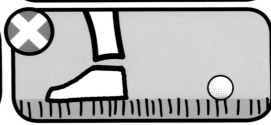

16-1 General (f) Playing Stroke While Another Ball in Motion

The player shall not play a stroke while another ball is in motion after a stroke from the putting green, except that, if a player does so, he incurs no penalty if it was his turn to play.

(Lifting ball interfering with or assisting play while another ball in motion – see Rule 22).

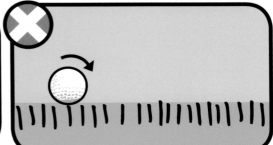

16-2 Ball Overhanging Hole

When any part of the ball overhangs the lip of the hole, the player is allowed enough time to reach the hole without unreasonable delay and an additional ten seconds to determine whether the ball is at rest. If by then the ball has not fallen into the hole, it is deemed to be at rest. If the ball subsequently falls into the hole, the player is deemed to have holed out with his last stroke, and he shall add a penalty stroke to his score for the hole; otherwise there is no penalty under this Rule.

(Undue delay – see Rule 6-7).

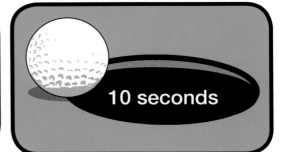

10 seconds

RULE 17:
The Flagstick

17 Definition - The Flagstick

The flagstick is a movable straight indicator, with or without bunting or other material attached, centred in the hole to show its position. It shall be circular in cross-section.

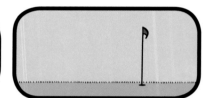

17-1 Flagstick Attended, Removed or Held Up

Before making a stroke, from anywhere on the course, the player may have the flagstick attended, removed or held up to indicate the position of the hole.

If the flagstick is not attended, removed or held up before the player makes a stroke, it must not be attended, removed or held up during the stroke or while the player's ball is in motion if doing so might influence the movement of the ball.

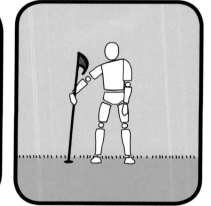

17-2 Unauthorised Attendance

If an opponent or his caddie in match play or a fellow-competitor or his caddie in stroke play, without the player's authority or prior knowledge, attends, removes or holds up the flagstick during the stroke or while the ball is in motion, and the act might influence the movement of the ball, the opponent or fellow-competitor incurs the applicable penalty.

In stroke play, if a breach of Rule 17-2 occurs and the competitor's ball subsequently strikes the flagstick, the person attending or holding it or anything carried by him, the competitor incurs no penalty. The ball is played as it lies except that, if the stroke was made on the putting green, the stroke is cancelled and the ball must be replaced and replayed.

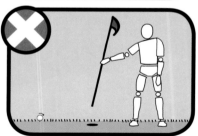

Penalty for Breach of Rule 17-1 or 17-2:

Match play – Loss of hole;
Stroke play – Two strokes.

17-3 Ball Striking Flagstick or Attendant

The player's ball shall not strike:

a. The flagstick when attended, removed or held up;
b. The person attending or holding up the flagstick or anything carried by him; or
c. The flagstick in the hole, unattended, when the stroke has been made on the putting green.

Exception

When the flagstick is attended, removed or held up without the player's authority – see Rule 17-2.

Penalty for Breach of Rule 17-3:

Match play – Loss of hole;
Stroke play – Two strokes, and the ball shall be played as it lies.

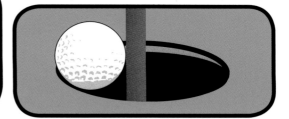

17-4 Ball Resting Against Flagstick

When a player's ball rests against the flagstick in the hole and the ball is not holed, the player or another person authorised by him may move or remove the flagstick, and if the ball falls into the hole, the player is deemed to have holed out with his last stroke; otherwise, the ball, if moved, must be placed on the lip of the hole, without penalty.

RULE 21: Cleaning Ball

21 Cleaning Ball

A ball on the putting green may be cleaned when lifted under Rule 16-1b. Elsewhere, a ball may be cleaned when lifted, except when it has been lifted:

a. To determine if it is unfit for play (Rule 5-3);
b. For identification (Rule 12-2), in which case it may be cleaned only to the extent necessary for identification; or
c. Because it is assisting or interfering with play (Rule 22).

If a player cleans his ball during play of a hole except as provided in this Rule, he incurs a penalty of one stroke and the ball, if lifted must be replaced.

If a player who is required to replace a ball fails to do so, he incurs the general penalty under the applicable Rule, but there is no additional penalty under Rule 21.

Exception

If a player incurs a penalty for failing to act in accordance with Rule 5-3, 12-2 or 22, there is no additional penalty under Rule 21.

RULE 25: Abnormal Ground Conditions, Embedded Ball and Wrong Putting Green

25-1 Abnormal Ground Conditions (a) Interference

Interference by an abnormal ground condition occurs when a ball lies in or touches the condition or when the condition interferes with the player's stance or the area of his intended swing. If the player's ball lies on the putting green, interference also occurs if an abnormal ground condition on the putting green intervenes on his line of putt. Otherwise, intervention on the line of play is not, of itself, interference under this Rule.

25-1 Abnormal Ground Conditions (b) Relief

Except when the ball is in a water hazard or a lateral water hazard, a player may take relief from interference by an abnormal ground condition as follows:

i. Through the Green: If the ball lies through the green, the player must lift the ball and drop it, without penalty, within one club-length of and not nearer the hole than the nearest point of relief. The nearest point of relief must not be in a hazard or on a putting green. When the ball is dropped within one club-length of the nearest point of relief, the ball must first strike a part of the course at a spot that avoids interference by the condition and is not in a hazard and not on a putting green.

ii. In a Bunker: If the ball is in a bunker, the player must lift the ball and drop it either:

    a. Without penalty, in accordance with Clause (i) above except that the nearest point of relief must be in the bunker and the ball must be dropped in the bunker or, if complete relief is impossible, as near as possible to the spot where the ball lay, but not nearer the hole, on a part of the course in the bunker that affords maximum available relief from the condition; or

    b. Under penalty of one stroke, outside the bunker keeping the point where the ball lay directly between the hole and the spot on which the ball is dropped, with no limit to how far behind the bunker the ball may be dropped.

iii. On the Putting Green: If the ball lies on the putting green, the player must lift the ball and place it, without penalty, at the nearest point of relief that is not in a hazard or, if complete relief is impossible, at the nearest point to where it lay that affords maximum available relief from the condition, but not nearer the hole and not in a hazard. The nearest point of relief or maximum available relief may be off the putting green.

iv. On the Teeing Ground: If the ball lies on the teeing ground, the player must lift the ball and drop it, without penalty, in accordance with Clause (i) above.

The ball may be cleaned when lifted under Rule 25-1b. (Ball rolling to a position where there is interference by the condition from which relief was taken – see Rule 20-2c(v)).

Exception

A player may not take relief under this Rule if (a) it is clearly unreasonable for him to make a stroke because of interference by anything other than an abnormal ground condition or (b) interference by an abnormal ground condition would occur only through use of an unnecessarily abnormal stance, swing or direction of play.

NOTE 1

If a ball is in a water hazard (including a lateral water hazard), the player is not entitled to relief, without penalty, from interference by an abnormal ground condition. The player must play the ball as it lies (unless prohibited by Local Rule) or proceed under Rule 26-1.

NOTE 2

If a ball to be dropped or placed under this Rule is not immediately recoverable, another ball may be substituted.

25-3 Wrong Putting Green
(a) Interference

Interference by a wrong putting green occurs when a ball is on the wrong putting green.

Interference to a player's stance or the area of his intended swing is not, of itself, interference under this Rule.

25-3 Wrong Putting Green
(b) Relief

If a player's ball lies on a wrong putting green, he must not play the ball as it lies. He must take relief, without penalty, as follows:

The player must lift the ball and drop it within one club-length of and not nearer the hole than the nearest point of relief. The nearest point of relief must not be in a hazard or on a putting green. When dropping the ball within one club-length of the nearest point of relief, the ball must first strike a part of the course at a spot that avoids interference by the wrong putting green and is not a hazard and not on a putting green. The ball may be cleaned when lifted under this Rule.

Penalty for Breach of Rule:

Match play – Loss of hole; Stroke play – Two strokes.

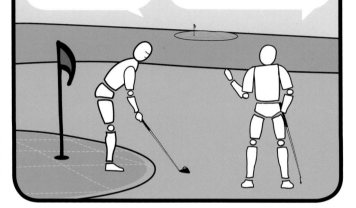

As I'm standing on this green to play my shot can I take relief?

I'm afraid not. Relief from a putting green may only be taken if your ball is on the green not just your stance.

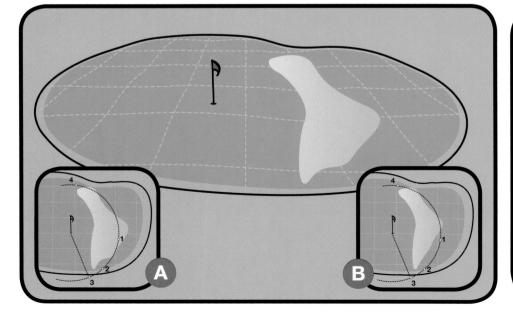

Casual Water on Putting Green

In both illustrations the player's ball lies on the putting green at Point 1. In illustration **A** his ball is in casual water, while in illustration **B** casual water intervenes on his line of putt, in either case, if relief is required, the player must place the ball at Point 3, the 'nearest point of relief' even though it is not on the putting green. Point 2 is the 'nearest point of relief' but the water still intervenes with his line of putt. Point 4 may be on the green, but it is not the nearest point of relief.

Andrew's

golf.co.uk

ETIQUETTE

ETIQUETTE (in short)

on the green...

Things we feel you should know

Don't move, talk or stand close to a player making a stroke, or make a shadow.

Don't step on the line of another players putt.

Always play without delay, leave the putting green as soon as all the players have holed out.

Trolleys and bags must not be taken on the putting green.

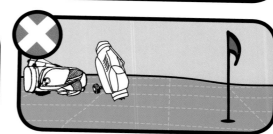

Carefully lift flagstick straight up out of hole and carefully replace, avoiding damage to hole.

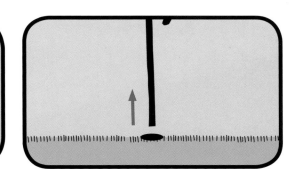

You may repair ball marks and old hole plugs on the line of your putt, including spike marks, but not any other damage. (Rule 16-1c).

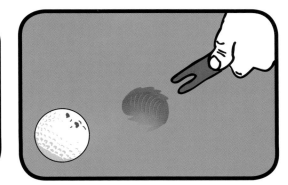

You may mark, lift and clean your ball, on the putting green. Always replace it on the exact spot. (Rule 16-1b).

Don't test the putting surface by scraping it or rolling a ball over it. (Rule 16-1d).

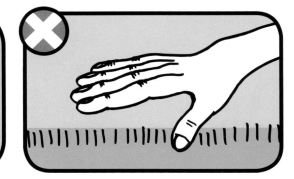

A player may not repair spike mark damage if it might subsequently assist him.

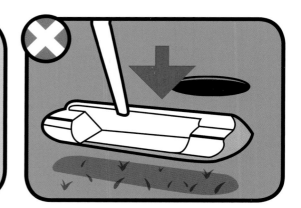

A player may move his ball marker if it is on another players line – usually moved a putter head away to the side. Remember to replace your marker, otherwise you will be penalised for playing from the wrong place. (Rule 20-7).

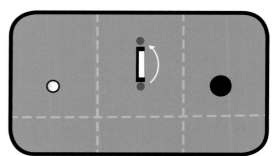

You may hold the flagstick while putting providing it is lifted from the hole, and the ball does not strike it. (Rule 17-3a). A player may not use the flagstick to steady himself. (Rule 14-3).

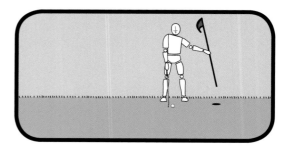

A player may have the flag attended or removed even if his ball is not on the putting surface. (Rule 17-1).

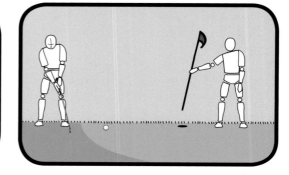

The person who is furthest away plays first, irrespective of whether they are on the green or not.

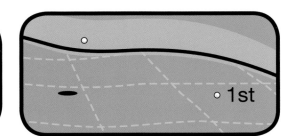

A player may remove loose impediments with his hand or cap, providing he does not push anything down. (Rule 16-1a).

You may adjust the flagstick so that it is centred, you may not however, adjust it so that it is leaning away from you.

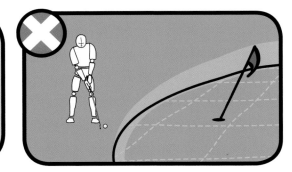

You may move the flagstick that has already been removed if it may influence the movement of the ball.

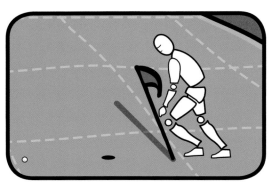

Andrew's GOLF TUITION BOOKS

- How to hold a golf club
- How to aim at the target
- The correct posture
- The half swing
- The full swing
- What equipment to buy
- About a golf course
- Basic rules
- How to score and the function of the golf handicap
- About a score card

- The roll of the ball
- How to hold a putter
- The correct posture
- How to aim at the target
- The putting stroke
- How to read a green
- What putters to buy
- About a modern green
- Rules of the putting green

COMING SOON

- Pitch and chip like a pro
- Club selection
- Grip position
- How to read the green
- Distance control
- Lob shots
- Chip and run shots
- Recovery shots
- Bunkers in detail
- Rules

Visit www.andrewsgolf.co.uk • Email: info@andrewsgolf.co.uk